PRAISE

John has poured his heart and soul into this book. It a from the depths of his personal experiences, both highs and lows. John's genuine commitment to Christ comes through loud and clear. I strongly recommend that you get your copy and enjoy every page of this interesting read.

JIMMIE KEELING THSCA HALL OF FAME
RETIRED COACH OF 60 PLUS YEARS
LEGENDARY HARDIN-SIMMONS HEAD
FOOTBALL COACH

John Ward had already "signed on" with the Lord when we met some 30 years ago. His zeal for the Lord, regard for others and dogged desire to live a life of service were evident from the "git-go", and he had been on that up-and-down road as he coached, taught, witnessed and preached the Word of God.

I know no one who doesn't love and respect this warrior for God. The almighty One got his attention with a recent disease that almost took him out, but John emerged on the other side, determined to fill each day with full acknowledgement of the Lord, including a heartfelt compulsion to write a book!

"Heartfelt" is a good word to describe John Ward. Look into his eyes and see all the way to his soul. "I'm a coach." he says. "Not an author." With his assessment of himself. I generally agree - a grammarian he "ain't"!

But there's no mistaking his dogged determination to serve the Lord daily. Folks whose children play football for John Ward will indeed be molded to be "more like the Master". If I had a son, I'd want him to be coached by John Ward. Reading his book will help you understand why.

DON NEWBURY CHANCELLOR - HOWARD PAYNE UNIVERSITY

100-0

COACH JOHN WARD

Clear Fork Publishing

100-0

Copyright © 2021 by Coach John Ward

ALL RIGHTS RESERVED. NO PART OF THIS BOOK MAY BE REPRODUCED IN ANY FORM OR BY ANY ELECTRONIC OR MECHANICAL MEANS INCLUDING INFORMATION STORAGE AND RETRIEVAL SYSTEMS - EXCEPT IN THE CASE OF BRIEF QUOTATIONS EMBODIED IN CRITICAL ARTICLES OR REVIEWS - WITHOUT PERMISSION IN WRITING FROM ITS PUBLISHER, CLEAR FORK PUBLISHING.

Summary: This book is the story of my life before salvation and after salvation and the journey of 100-0, physically dying. I am praying this book will speak to everyone, no matter what job, church, occupation, or situations. Brokenness is a powerful and unpleasant journey,
but most intimate journey with Jesus.

Clear Fork Publishing

P.O. Box 870 102 S. Swenson

Stamford, Texas 79553 (915) 209-0003

www.clearforkpublishing.com

Printed in the United States of America

Softcover ISBN - 978-1-950169-79-5

CONTENTS

Preface	ix
Introduction	xi
1. Before Jesus Christ	1
2. Salvation	10
3. After Salvation	13
4. 100-0 (Oil Bowl)	21
5. Zero "o"-Dead Physically	25
6. Rise Up	32
7. God is in Control	39
8. Overflow	44
9. Transformation	51
10. Victory Living	58
11. The Miracle	62
12. Purpose+Passion	68
13. God is so Good-All the Time He is Good	81
About the Author	85

Poach (Preacher/Coach-Teacher)

Philippians 1:21 New International Version (NIV)
[21] *For to me, to live is Christ and to die is gain.*

John 16:33 New International Version (NIV)

33 "I have told you these things, so that in me you may have peace. In this world you will have trouble. But take heart! I have overcome the world."

James 1:2-4 New International Version (NIV)

2 Consider it pure joy, my brothers and sisters, [a] whenever you face trials of many kinds, **3** because you know that the testing of your faith produces perseverance. **4** Let perseverance finish its work so that you may be mature and complete, not lacking anything.

INTRODUCTION

As I am thinking about putting this book in writing. Our world is going through the greatest challenge of Covid-19. States are closed, towns are closed, and schools are closed, and have 6.6 million people applying for unemployment. Wow, what uncertain and challenging times. A lot of brokenness and rough times and more to come. I am reminded of these scriptures:

---

2 Chronicles 7:14 New International Version (NIV)

14 if my people, who are called by my name, will humble themselves and pray and seek my face and turn from their wicked ways, then I will hear from heaven, and I will forgive their sin and will heal their land.

The Holy Spirit has been tugging on me to write this

book. God has allowed through this tough time to have time to write this book.

This book is the story of my life before salvation and after salvation and the journey of 100-0, physically dying and being face to face with this set of scriptures.

Romans 12:1-2 New International Version (NIV)
A Living Sacrifice
12 Therefore, I urge you, brothers and sisters, in view of God's mercy, to offer your bodies as a living sacrifice, holy and pleasing to God—this is your true and proper worship. **²** Do not conform to the pattern of this world, but be transformed by the renewing of your mind. Then you will be able to test and approve what God's will is—his good, pleasing and perfect will.

I am praying this book will speak to everyone, no matter what job, church, occupation, or situations. Brokenness is a powerful and unpleasant journey, but most intimate journey with Jesus. God showed me that our journey relationship with God has many valleys, suffering, mountain tops, and heart pulling out times, but God is always faithful and desires all of us, not 99% or 50% or 80 %, God wants us totally surrendered to Him. We may think we are giving God everything, but we are till it gets uncomfortable. God is faithful and will at all time use time, situations, and circumstances to strip our pride and self out of the way, so we can be all in for Jesus. Praise Jesus for all the suffering in my life and giving me the strength, courage, and honor to experience my journey in life for Jesus Christ. Jesus gets all the Glory and Praise!!! It's not an accident that you are reading this book, God has something to show you and help grow you in your walk with God.

ONE
BEFORE JESUS CHRIST

I was born December 29, 1969, in El Paso, Texas, my father is Gerald D. Ward and mother is Margo Ward. My dad was in the army for 27 years and mother a waitress for 37 years. I have one brother Don Ward, he is 2 years older than me. My parents divorced when I was 9 years old, my dad, at the time was stationed in Korea and almost ready to go home. It was devastating for me and my brother, it tore our hearts out. My mother took us to San Antonio, Tx, we moved to governmental housing, it was a tough time. My mom worked 2-3 jobs, she left at 5:00 a.m. and came home at 1:00 a.m., she was a waitress and hair dresser.

My mother would come in no matter how late and wake me and my brother up and lavish us with kisses and tell us how much she loved us and that we could do anything if we work hard for it. So, me and my brother had lots of time on our hands, my mom showed us how to do laundry, clean house, and cook food. Well, we ended up learning a lot by trial and error. We ended up moving to a nice apartment complex and a good area, when I was entering 6th grade. Me and my brother got jobs doing paper routes to all the apartment complexes in the area, it kept us busy.

I remember me and other so-called friends, went into the Mr. M, by the apartment complex we lived in. My friends started stuffing their pockets with candy and asked me to do the same, I knew it was wrong but ended up doing it too. The owner caught me going out the door, he took me to his office and made me empty my pockets, I was so scared and felt so sad. The owner got after me pretty good and then told me, "he thought I was a great kid", and gave me a job at the store. Thus, every day after I got done with school, I would go help stock and all different duties. I am so thankful for him. I believe that was God's Hand on me then. My dad came back from Korea midway my 5th grade year, it was so awesome to see him. Well, at the end of my sixth-grade year, me and my brother decided to go live with my dad in Lawton, Oklahoma. A long drive from San Antonio, Texas to Lawton, Oklahoma.

As a little pudgy 7th grader in Lawton, Oklahoma, I decided to play 7th grade football, Oklahoma had 2-a-days in 7th Grade to 12th Grade. Wow, it was murder for a city boy that was used to drinking chocolate milk and eating ice cream sitting around watching television all the time. I remember the coaches making us do 100-yard bear crawls at the end of practice, the only thing that saved me, was the 7-11 sign I could see down the road from the field. I knew I was going to get a big gulp after practice, for the 3-mile bike ride home. When athletics was brought into my life, I developed a love for workouts and the sport of football, wrestling, and all sports. I lost all the baby fat and trimmed up, I was so excited. But at the time, my family life was very tough, both my dad and step mother were alcoholics. It was always chaotic at home, very negative, and hated seeing my dad in turmoil. So, me and my brother went fishing and stayed away from the house most of the time.

One summer, we had nothing to do, I saw a sub-division being built next door to the trailer park we lived in. I told my brother, I was going to go over to the sub division and find a job. I went over there, and the 2nd person I talked to was a big man named Smokey Tolbert, he was the owner of the sub division and many others, in Lawton, Oklahoma. Smokey hired me and my brother to clean streets and other duties on the weekends (10 hours a day-2 dollar an hour), he would pick us up early and bring us back late. He became our big brother, he was an awesome man, he showed us how to open a bank account and took us out to eat at country clubs and everywhere. I believe God put him in our lives for a big reason. I also was able to open a lawn business in the big trailer park we lived in, and made a lot of spare money.

My dad retired from the army, after a year and a half, and we moved to Huntsville, Texas. Huntsville is a beautiful place, huge pine trees, and many prisons. My dad became the health administer in one of the prisons. I had to finish my 8th grade year at Huntsville, I was an outsider and I got into a fight every other day, till everyone knew I wasn't going to back down. Our family life was still chaotic, but me and my brother were so busy that we were never home much. I was a shy nerd type kid till my 9th grade year, I became the outgoing, love everyone, class clown, and got everyone to love the jock kid.

After my freshman year, my dad moved back to Korea and my best friend's parents, took me in for all of my high school years. Harry and Bobby Sturgeon are an awesome family, they have come to every major event in my life and my family's life. They have always been there for me. After my freshman year, I got lazy in my academics and just coasted through school, I worked 2 different jobs to make it, and did what I wanted when I wanted. My goal was to play college football, I had a great senior year in football and ended up getting a 2-year scholarship to play football at Kilgore Jr. College, because I didn't have the grades. I was in the last quarter of my class ranking and didn't care about my academics.

I ended up playing football at Kilgore Junior College, I straightened up in the academic department, my grades became priority. Monday through Thursday, from 6:00 p.m. to 10:00p.m., was dedicated to my studies. My first semester was all remedial classes and didn't count, I committed to my school work daily. During the first semester, my reading teacher told me to see her at the end of class. She told me that my reading level was at the 6th grade level and told me that I would never graduate from college or needed to go take up a trade job, like welding or work force. My heart sank, but I straightened up and told the teacher that I will work harder and that I was going to graduate from college and get my master's degree. I was going to be a teacher and a coach.

My history professor was a major influence in my time at Kilgore Junior College, his name was Mr. Strout, an ex-drill sergeant at Paris Island, during Vietnam. The first day of class, he through the text book out the window and said for us to take great notes and assigned four books for us to read, and one of the books was," The Rumor of War", Wow, thick book. I could read ok, but I would think about eating a cheeseburger while I was reading it and wouldn't remember the main idea. Thus, every night I would read a chapter in the "Rumor of War", book, I would read a paragraph and then write down the main idea. When all my buddies and friends went out, I would do my studies from 6:00 p.m. to 10:00 p.m., they would laugh at me, but I knew what I had to do.

After a month, I began to remember what I was reading and fell in love with reading books. After the first year of college, I had a 3.00 GPA, and was ready for my 2nd year. Football was going well, ended up playing a lot and starting a couple of games my freshman year. I loved the game of football, the competition. The summer before my sophomore year, I was living in Fredericksburg, Texas and doing the summer strength and conditioning program and training a young man named Tracie Williams. I lived with the wonderful family and helped with their janitorial business —The Williams Family. They were awesome people, God had his hand on this situation as well. About 2 weeks before I reported to 3 a day workout at Kilgore Junior College, my defensive line coach called me and told me that the coaches wanted me to be an assistant coach and not play football that year.

Well, I told them that I wanted to play and was having a great summer of preparation. I reported in to summer workouts, I was last on the depth chart and was put in the visitor locker Room on a hook, away from my teammates. It tore my heart out, but my teammates helped me move forward, I just told myself every evening to work harder and great things will happen. After the first day, I was moved to third on the defensive depth chart. Second day, I was moved to second on the depth chart. On the Third day, the evening practice, I was on starting defense for our team defensive segment, and it was like I ended up making every tackle, and the team was chanting Animal(nickname). It was so awesome.

Coach Jim Miller, Head Football Coach, brought us together and prayed, "Please protect us from the animal and forgive me for the way I have treated him", and I can't remember the rest of the prayer. After Amen, Coach Miller grabbed all my equipment, I tried to tell coach that I could carry it, He told me no I got it, He told me that, "I will never doubt you again", He took me to the locker room and kicked out a freshman and put me in a locker with my teammates and I started every game that year. We ended up playing in the Shrine Bowl in Tyler, we lost by 3 points. What an awesome year, I forgot to tell ya'll. All the sophomores before the year met and set standards and goals for the season. There was 17 of us, we set a curfew during the week and made mandatory study hall in our rooms Monday - Thursday, from 6:00 p.m. to 10:00 p.m. We had 38 freshman report in and everyone of them except one had a great sophomore year.

The one, was named Rodney Williams, from Jasper, Texas. He was an amazing young man, tremendous athlete and was tall and strong. We played on the defensive line next to each other. He would always come by my dorm and we would talk about grades and football and other things in life. One morning, Rodney came over and we were talking about the next year, and Rodney said," He was going to be all American the next year". We had a great time cutting up about life. That night, I was coming home from the movies, and there was an ambulance in front of his dorm. He hung himself in the shower. This tore my heart out, I couldn't understand, I had just seen him that morning. I kept asking myself, what was he thinking, what could I have done to help him. This shook my life, I didn't know how fragile life is and the power of influence we have. I asked myself if there was something I could have done. It was a rough and tough situation, but I believe God got my attention at that time.

After the Shrine Bowl, I enrolled at Austin College to play my last two years and coach and get my master's. I was working in Fredericksburg, Tx, at Mr. Gattis, I just closed and got home at 3:00 a.m. in the morning. I got a call at 7:00 a.m. in the morning, from Bill Anderson, the head football coach, at Howard Payne University. He said that his son was coming to pick me up at 7:30 a.m., I told him that I was already committed to another college, he told me that I was supposed to be at Howard Payne University. So, at 7:30 a.m., I went with Bobby Anderson to Brownwood, Tx, to Howard Payne University.

That morning, I am sitting in Bill Anderson's Office, Coach Anderson is a big man, he had bi-focal glasses on and leaned over his desk and tells me, "John, you are a Howard Payne Yellow Jacket, God has put you on my heart. I told him, "No, Sir", I have committed to Austin College. Coach Anderson said, you will see and he took me to the team meeting and introduced me to the team and next thing I know, I go back and get my stuff and enroll at Howard Payne University and sitting in a dorm room. I believe God was in this too.

For the first month, I lived the name "animal", lived the wild college life. I was working out in the weight room and I met the David in my life. David Arcos, a short dude, that had a light glowing from him. I can't explain it, I was working out and being loud with a bunch of bad language, when David approached me and introduced himself. David told me he liked the way I expressed myself and invited me to a drama meeting. I thought that this would be something about me, I came to the meeting and they were praying, so I bolted to get out of the room and David introduced me to everyone and showered me with love and hospitality. I started hanging out with the Christian drama team, they where goofy, but they had a joy that didn't come from a beer and party seen. Then I started performing Christian drama at different youth groups.

February 14, 1990-The drama team performed at Bangs First Baptist Church, and then we went to Mims Auditorium at Howard Payne University, the group New Songs were performing. Man, they can sing, all through the concert I felt something weird in my heart. At the end of the concert, the lead singer leads the invitation, I had a lump in my throat and my heart was pounding out of my chest. I tried everything in my life to get peace, nothing worked, I needed Jesus Christ. So, I accepted Jesus into my Heart. The lead singer asked us to come to the front, I gripped the seats in front of me and wiggled and wanted to go, but didn't. The invitation felt like it went on and on for an hour, then the lead singer looked at me in the dark auditorium and said, "it's your time big boy", I ran down to the alter and cried like a baby and cried out to Jesus. I felt all burdens in my life leave me and I had a joy that can't be explained.

Romans 10:9 New International Version (NIV)

[9] If you declare with your mouth, "Jesus is Lord," and believe in your heart that God raised him from the dead, you will be saved.

2 Corinthians 5:17 New International Version (NIV)

[17] Therefore, if anyone is in Christ, the new

creation has come:[a] The old has gone, the new is here!

I didn't sleep the whole night!!! Jesus, Jesus, so excited that I became a child of God, all old things in my life where wiped away by the blood of Jesus, and I became a new creation.

TWO

SALVATION

February 14, 1990-That is when I began my new journey, as a child of God, a new creation of Christ. My life was transformed, I had a filthy mouth, God took that away from me first. I had a peace that passive all understanding, a joy that was unexplainable. I was on fire for Jesus, couldn't stop talking about Jesus and told everyone I met, how great and loving is Jesus. God blessed me with five true Christian friends that held me accountable: Bob Canfield, Chawn Cummings, Mike Rodgers, Ray Archiga, and Brent Franklin. We all went to Howard Payne University together and spent a lot of time with them. We served in FCA, state school ministry, and many other Godly things.

The spring semester, God grew me and my excitement for Jesus was like a river, fast flowing with Gods love. I went to spend the summer in Fredericksburg, Tx. When I got there, God had another plan, I ended up going to Wichita Falls, Tx and spent the summer with my dad. I went there on fire for Jesus, started working for a temporary service, ended up a great friendship with my supervisor and he asked me to go to a club and I told him I loved Jesus, I couldn't do that, but he told me I could still go and not drink and hang out. I ended going and went back to the old ways of drinking and partying. During that time, God gave me a desire to seek and read God's Word. My brother came to visit, we went out and got drunk and we went back home and, on my bed, was a Bible opened and this verse was highlighted.

Matthew 6:24 New International Version (NIV)

[24] "No one can serve two masters. Either you will hate the one and love the other, or you will be devoted to the one and despise the other. You cannot serve both God and money.

I read the verse, and instantly became sober and cried all night long and my brother thought I was crazy. I told him, I was straddling the fence as a Christian, I was Praising Jesus and then loving the world. God grabbed my heart and showed me I need to be sold out in my walk with God. Thus, my life transformed from that time on.

Romans 12:1-2 New International Version (NIV)

A Living Sacrifice

12 Therefore, I urge you, brothers and sisters, in view of God's mercy, to offer your bodies as a living sacrifice, holy and pleasing to God—this is your true and proper worship. [2] Do not conform to the pattern of this world, but be transformed by the renewing of your mind. Then you will be able to test and approve what God's will is—his good, pleasing and perfect will.

I learned that God called me not to love Him with half my life, God wanted all of me.

Mark 12:30-31 New International Version (NIV)

[30] Love the Lord your God with all your heart and with all your soul and with all your mind and with all your strength.'[a] [31] The second is this: 'Love your neighbor as yourself.'[b] There is no commandment greater than these."

I learned how important it was to spend time with God daily. Thus, being a Christian, it's all about our relationship with God. Loving God with everything in our life.

THREE
AFTER SALVATION

Romans 8:18 New International Version (NIV)
Present Suffering and Future Glory
¹⁸ I consider that our present sufferings are not worth comparing with the glory that will be revealed in us.

After understanding that being a Christian or Child of God, means to have a daily relationship with God. Meditating on Gods Word and praying without ceasing. It hasn't been a rose garden. Me and my family have been through deep-deep rugged valleys and broken times, but we thank God for every minute of it. Because God has transformed us through those times. Think about it, if you didn't have hard times, then you would not have grit. Grit is deep character to respond to Jesus and trust God through the good, bad, and ugly.

First, my junior year of playing football at Howard Payne University, started out as an awesome year. About the 5th game of the season, I started feeling fatigued all the time, but I fought it and kept going. My game film started looking like I was taking plays off, it killed me to watch. On a Monday night, I nearly passed out in practice, and found out I had a severe case of mono. They put me on bed rest, which was tough because football was my life. Then God opened the door up to be the FCA President, I was so nervous, but God molded me and showed me that I am not in control. God is in control, football is not my god, only Jesus is my Lord and Savior. God blessed me so much to be able to serve through FCA.

God opened up so many doors to minister. God put on my heart to have a ministry called FFC (Fools for Christ), it was a branch off of FCA, it was so awesome. We ended up performing all over and God allowed us to minister at the state school and many youth groups. It looked like a broken and no hope situation that I missed half the football season, but God was bigger. Then at a Thanksgiving dinner at Early First Baptist, I met my wife, Jan Ward, man-Wow, what a woman. When our eyes met, I knew she was the one. My senior season went great, God grew me daily closer to Him. That spring, I asked Jan Ward to marry me, and she said yes. I proposed to her at an FFC family rally at the Baptist Encampment, at Brownwood Lake.

That summer, God opened doors to go with Athletes in Action, a summer retreat, in Fort Collins, CO. We learned how to share word of God and evangelize. I will never forget that summer, it was such a test to be away from Jan. We had to have a job and did bible study every evening 6:00 p.m. to 10:00 p.m. The summer was an awesome time of growth in my walk with God, I learned how to witness and one-on-one sharing of Christ. The Athletes in Action Staff for the first month, trained us to outreach, and then they left 37 of us to run the show. We took our walk with God to our jobs, workouts, and everything. God put me in charge of outreach, it was a transforming experience that made me into a more Christlike Servant.

When I got back, I started coaching at Howard Payne University, coached the defensive line under the New Head Coach Vance Gibson, and Defensive Coordinator Phil Fuller. It was an awesome year, I got to do the FCA, FFC, State School Ministry, and coach. We ended up winning the conference championship and going to the national NAIA Division II Play-offs. Got married the week after the football season ended, December 12, 1992, it was one of the happiest days of my life. I praise Jesus for Howard Payne University, I got to live behind Dr. Don Newbury, in private apartments. It was awesome, Dr. Newbury treated us like his sons, he prayed for us and took care of us. He is a dear friend and brother in Christ to this day. He is an amazing Christian Man and his family is unbelievable. As for the professors at Howard Payne University, God gave them major patience with me, Dr. Roth, Dr. Jack Stanfield, Dr. Bird, and Dr. Smith and many more shaped me and prepared me for my occupation and life.

After Howard Payne University, God led us to Hardin-Simmons University to work on my Master's Degree and coach with Coach Jimmie Keeling (my mentor). My father-in-law asked me how I was going to take care of his daughter and my response was, "God will take care of us", I don't think I got any bonus points with him with that response. We moved to Abilene, TX, lived in marriage housing, on Vogel Street, no AC and no jobs, and no idea what we were about to do. This was the first week of June, that Monday, I started my master's classes and got a job at a landscaping company working from 2:00 p.m. till dark. My wife was thinking what in the world did I get myself into, I don't see my husband.

We went the first night without AC in Summer weather in Abilene, Wow, and the next day, the director of the campus housing felt sorry for us and gave us a window unit, for our bedroom, Praise Jesus-Praise Jesus!!! Two weeks before football 2-a-days started, we went to the human resources department, there was people everywhere, I asked them why there were so many people, they told me everyone was applying for a UPS job. I prayed and applied for it, and waited two hours for an interview, the guy that interviewed me asked why I applied for the job, 206 people are interviewing for this same job. I spilled my heart to him, I felt God was leading me to work for UPS and told him my situation.

The next day, UPS called me to offer me the job. God is so Good, back then ten dollars an hour was big thing in 1994. I worked from 3:00 a.m. to 9:00 a.m. Monday thru Friday, went to school and then coached till 7:00 or 8:00 p.m. and games on Saturday. Me and Jan had date night at the fieldhouse during football season, I cut the game film and Jan helped do the laundry. We look back and laugh and we really had a good time together. Coach Keeling showed me how to be a Christian Coach, and to lead a Christian Football Program. Coach Keeling everyday was a free coaching clinic daily, he and his wife Susan where always there for me and Jan. Jimmie Keeling from then till this present time, has mentored me and been there for me. He has taught me more than he will ever know, on how to be a man of God. I was taught how to care for staff and players, organization, coach defense and offense, and off-season program.

One of the greatest experiences in my life. Jan and I lead the FCA Huddle at Hardin-Simmons, and taught University morning Sunday school at church. It was a busy, but an awesome time for me and Jan. Our 1994 Football Season was awesome, we ended up winning the conference championship and got beat in the semi-final game against Westminster (10-0), Wow, what a game. That spring, I ended up getting a job, in Cooper TX, at Cooper ISD, with Joey Florence. Him being another great Christian man and coach that I learned so much from him. I had some great years at Cooper, we were so blessed. God Blessed us with a great church, Klondike First Baptist, great coaching staff and awesome school district, and wonderful community.

My oldest daughter was born on January 22, 1996, in Sulphur Springs, TX, during my 2nd year at Cooper, TX. We were rocking along and Satan attacked my family. Satan attacked my marriage, I was worried about being a coordinator and climbing the coaching ladder, and put my wife second. Satan worked his way into our marriage, and I saw the warning signs of Satan, but my selfishness and pride blinded me. Boom, my life changed one October evening, and she and Lauren went back to Brownwood, Tx, to live with her parents.

Those six months was an overflow of humility, I hit the bottom of life, every time I walked by Lauren's room, my heart pulled out of my chest and when I woke up and Jan wasn't beside me in bed. All I had was Jesus, every day I had to read the bible to be able to go to work. God gave me the strength to finish the football season, every weekend I went to Brownwood to see Lauren and Jan. Very tough time, before Christmas, I experienced massive nose bleeds, that lasted 30 minutes to an hour. I went to the doctor and was diagnosed with sinus infection, but I kept having nose bleeds. I started having fever and feeling very bad, I went to the nose and throat specialist, and he told me I was going into emergency surgery. He told me I had an abscess in my sinuses by my brain. I told the doctor I needed to coach in a basketball tournament, Coaches Wow!

I ended up having surgery and spent 2 nights in the hospital, and finally got out the day we got out for Christmas Break. Coach Florence met with me and told me to find a way to get my family back and he and the superintendent would work everything out. Thus, during Christmas break I looked for a job in the area, I was interviewing for a job at the state school when the principal at the alternative school at Brownwood called me and said to come talk to her after the interview. God ended up making me the lead teacher for 9th grade in the alternative center, I was the third teacher in only a few months. A challenge, but that spring, I learned so much and helped me to become a better teacher and coach. God is so Good. I thank God for Mrs. Adams the principal, she was an awesome Christian lady and administer.

God brought Jan and I back together, it was a rough road, I had to learn how to love my wife the way God called me to love her. I was broken, but God developed in me and Jan a love that was unbreakable. We have been married for 27 years and counting. I am telling you about this time in our life, because life is rough and tough, no matter if you are a Christian or not. But as Christians, God never leaves us or forsakes us, and if we are steadfast on him daily, great and unbelievable things can be accomplished. Jan and I being married is a miracle of God. God knew and used the brokenness to check our individual faith and relationship with God, and restored us and made us both more Christlike.

Matthew 5:45 New International Version (NIV)

⁴⁵ that you may be children of your Father in heaven. He causes his sun to rise on the evil and the good, and sends rain on the righteous and the unrighteous.

God opened up doors to coach at Brownwood ISD, with Coach Steve Freeman, I coached for 9 years there with a tremendous staff(Darren Allman, John Walsh, Mitch Moore, Mitch Stovall, Roby Clark, Charles Copeland, Andy Howard, Clay Coston, and many more), we had great seasons and I learned so much from Steve Freeman and staff about loving kids, treating coaches right , work ethic, organization of an athletic program, and how to treat people, and of course football.

At Brownwood, Dallas Huston plugged me in to supply preaching in the brown county area, it was awesome. Then, God opened up doors to be a bi-vocational pastor at Sunset Mission in Brownwood, TX. Brother Henson, Pastor at First Baptist Church, licensed to be a pastor. Then, I bi-vocational pastored at Gustine First Baptist and they ordained me as a pastor. God overflowed many great brothers and sisters of Christ, in our life that sharpened us as Christians and a Family. Also, my youngest daughter Kristi Elizabeth Ward was born at Brownwood Regional Hospital, on January 12, 1998. We were so Blessed in Brownwood from churches, staff, kids, school districts, and many other things. Thank you, Jesus, for that wonderful time.

I ended up getting my first head football coaching job in 2006, at DeLeon ISD. I was a head football coach and athletic director for the next 7 years at these different places (McKamy, Thrall, and Moody). God blessed us with great success and awesome staffs, kids, school districts, and communities. After that, I have been an assistant coach/teacher and bi-vocational pastor till the present. I am coaching/teaching at Stamford ISD and a bi-vocational pastor at Stamford First Baptist. I have been so blessed to be a coach for more than 25 years. God has blessed us immeasurably more than we deserve. We have been blessed to be in many communities all over Texas, we had to make family and stand up decisions many times, but we know God put us in every community for great reasons. We thank Jesus daily, for the people God has put into our life, from schools, churches, and communities. We know God provides, it may not be comfortable or peaceful at times, but God got us through it.

Ephesians 3:20 New International Version (NIV)

[20] Now to him who is able to do immeasurably more than all we ask or imagine, according to his power that is at work within us,

---

FOUR
100-0 (OIL BOWL)

Romans 12:1-2 New International Version (NIV)
   A Living Sacrifice
   12 Therefore, I urge you, brothers and sisters, in view of God's mercy, to offer your bodies as a living sacrifice, holy and pleasing to God—this is your true and proper worship. **²** Do not conform to the pattern of this world, but be transformed by the renewing of your mind. Then you will be able to test and approve what God's will is—his good, pleasing and perfect will

---

In 2017, we had an awesome football season at Stamford High School, we won the district championship and went three rounds deep, and had a ten-win season. This was my first-year coaching at Stamford, Wow, an awesome time and blessing to be a part of. That spring, Coach Casey asked me to coach with him at the Oil Bowl (All Star Football Game), a great opportunity, so blessed and flattered to be asked. I was excited about the opportunity. I didn't know what God was about to do in my life. God transformed me that 2018 summer.

Before school was out for the summer, I put the Oil Bowl defensive game plan together and started putting the plan into action. The Oil Bowl was June 16, 2018, coaches reported in, June 12, 2018, in the afternoon, all players, coaches and I on both sides. Great men, it was awesome to get to know all the other coaches from different schools. We met with the players and gave them the offensive and defensive game plans. Wednesday, we had two practices, God blessed us with great players, we practiced defense in the morning, the kids were glued in and we had a tremendous practice.

After practice, I felt numbness on the ends of my fingers and toes and some tingling. I just went on and hydrated, I was thinking I was just a little dehydrated. On Thursday, we had an awesome defensive practice again, the players picked it up quick. The Stamford Coaches done the defense, me (defensive coordinator), Coach Casey (Co-Head Coach) coached the secondary, Coach King coached the linebackers. It was just like another day at the office, we worked together like a machine. After the practices, the numbness and tingling in my fingers and toes persisted. I still was thinking it was just dehydration. That night, I started to feel bad, thought I was getting a sinus infection. I felt really tired, but it was a grinding week, getting everything ready. Friday morning, I was doing my devotional and the words where bouncing on the page and I had a hard time writing. Well, I went and took a shower and got dressed, I couldn't raise my legs to get dressed, my coordination was off.

It took me an hour to just get dressed. I went to breakfast and told Coach Casey, something was wrong, we went through symptoms and came up with dehydration again. We had one more practice, man it was hot. The numbness got worse and I continued to feel bad after practice, like I was ran over by a truck. That evening, we took teams to the basketball all-star games, we went to Wichita Falls Rider Gym. I had to take my time walking up bleachers, my legs would not cooperate. I was losing my balance, but just took my time and kept pressing forward. I felt worse and even more fatigued.

Saturday morning, Game Day, I couldn't write and couldn't read very long. I went to breakfast, I couldn't swallow my food and had a hard time even drinking water. We had a defensive walk-thru that morning, I went thru the game plan and last-minute adjustments. I noticed I couldn't yell like usual, I was losing my voice. When I would go up steps, I had to have help by bracing my knee with my arms and sitting down and getting up was tough as well. I was losing my strength. We went to the pre-game meal, I couldn't swallow anything by that time, I was staggering around and had a hard time standing or walking.

Our trainer, from Wichita Falls Hersey, examined me and told me to go to the emergency room. I told him I wanted to coach the game. He told me that I couldn't do that, I had fever and he knew something was wrong. God was looking out for me. Coach Casey and Coach King took me to the emergency room at the Wichita Falls Hospital. They had to drop me off, since they had to go get everyone ready for the game, my wife and daughter were on route to the hospital. The ER took me in and put me on IV's and did blood work. When my wife and daughter got to the hospital, the doctor released me with severe dehydration. I couldn't swallow or walk; my wife and daughter were very upset. They walked me to the car, my daughter drove me home to Stamford. I felt horrible and still wanted to go back and coach the game. I just wanted to coach those players, I felt I was letting everyone down.

When we got home, in Stamford, my wife and daughter helped me into the house and to my recliner. We got settled in, I felt horrible and couldn't swallow and spit in a big cup. I asked my wife and daughter to help me get up, so I could go to the bathroom. I tried to get up and fell to the floor. I couldn't move from my head to my toes, I was paralyzed. I could wiggle my toes, but I couldn't feel my fingers or toes. I told my daughter to call 911 and asked my wife to sit by me, I could think and talk. I told Jan, it was going to be a long road, something bad has happened, but God will get us through it. God is more powerful and bigger. The ambulance took me to Hendrick Medical Center. The journey began.

100-0

I was going 100 mph in my coaching and in life, I was going 100 mph as interim pastor at First Baptist Church Stamford. Life couldn't be any better. Then life changed in a second.

FIVE
ZERO "0"-DEAD PHYSICALLY

Philippians 1:21 New International Version (NIV)

²¹ For to me, to live is Christ and to die is gain.

When I got to the Emergency Room, at Hendrick Medical Center, in Abilene, Tx. They put me in an examination room and one or two neurologists were on hand. And within an hour they're where diagnosing as the Guillain-Barre Syndrome. The neurologist requested a spinal tap. They tried multiple times to do the spinal tap, but failed because three years ago, I had major back surgery, that fused my 4 and 5 lumbar vertebrates. It was like they had to go through a bunch of scaffolding. It was tough stuff, they sent me to a private room for the night. I had to have suction all night because I couldn't swallow.

I am telling you, we don't understand how much yucky stuff we swallow daily, wow, it was terrible. I didn't sleep the whole night, couldn't eat and felt like I was drowning in my own saliva. The next morning, the neurologist, Bonnie Hayashi, MD, she is an energetic and awesome neurologist, she came into my room and told me that, this morning she was no matter what going to get the spinal tap done to prove the diagnoses of the Guillain-Barre Syndrome. She summoned up about 5 nurses and nurses aids and they put me into the spinal tap position, it was rough, but through precision she got the spinal tap done. God's hand was upon Dr. Hayashi, I thank God for her persistence. With-in the next few hours, Dr. Hayashi came back and told me the diagnosis was right, that I needed to be in the ICU just in case I would have breathing problems. I still didn't know how to say or what Guillain-Barre syndrome was. I knew by the look on Jan's face, it was serious.

This is what Guillain-Barre Syndrome is:

Guillain-Barré (gee-YAH-buh-RAY)
 syndrome is a rare disorder in which
 your body's immune system attacks your
 nerves. Weakness and tingling in your
 extremities are usually the first
 symptoms.

These sensations can quickly spread, eventually paralyzing your whole body. In its most severe form Guillain-Barré syndrome is a medical emergency. Most people with the condition must be hospitalized to receive treatment.

The exact cause of Guillain-Barré syndrome is unknown. But it is often preceded by an infectious illness such as a respiratory infection or the stomach flu.

There's no known cure for Guillain-Barré syndrome, but several treatments can ease symptoms and reduce the duration of the illness. Most people recover from Guillain-Barré syndrome, though some may experience lingering effects from it, such as weakness, numbness or fatigue.

Symptoms

Guillain-Barré syndrome often begins with tingling and weakness starting in your feet and legs and spreading to your upper body and arms. In about half of people with the disorder, symptoms begin in the arms or face. As Guillain-Barré syndrome progresses, muscle weakness can evolve into paralysis.

SIGNS AND SYMPTOMS *of Guillain-Barré syndrome may include*:

- Prickling, pins and needles sensations in your fingers, toes, ankles or wrists
- Weakness in your legs that spreads to your upper body
- Unsteady walking or inability to walk or climb stairs
- Difficulty with eye or facial movements, including speaking, chewing or swallowing
- Severe pain that may feel achy or cramp like and may be worse at night
- Difficulty with bladder control or bowel function
- Rapid heart rate
- Low or high blood pressure
- Difficulty breathing

They made a port on my right lower side, by my hip, into a renal artery for plasmapheresis, and my breathing at this time was getting rough. I had to be put on a C-Pap machine to help me breath, with oxygen in my nose. Also, I had to have a suction tool, to suck out all the stuff in my mouth, or I would've suffocated. Well, during this time, people came from all around: local churches, church family, community members, coaches, players, and others from everywhere. They came to pray and give encouragement. Hundreds came through the ICU to see me and pray over me. I have clear memory of many but many I was in the blurry state not to remember. I remember all the pastors and youth ministers from Stamford coming and praying over me, I remember so many church families coming and praying over me and members from other churches, past coaches and players in my life, and other coaches from other schools.

My breathing kept getting worse, I couldn't sleep, I was in pain, and remember seeing the clock in the ICU, every second seemed like a day. My heart, at this time I am typing this, goes out to all the Covid-19 patients in ICU and on ventilators, I can't imagine not having any family there with me. I pray daily for everyone affected by this Covid-19, also pray for all medical staff, on the front lines. You don't know what all the nurses, doctors, and medical staff do, until you see it first-hand.

That Sunday, Father's Day, June 17, 2018, I was having a hard time breathing, and the nurses where checking on me frequently. Jan and David and Belinda Fernandez were with me when it was like I fell of the shelf, as far as my breathing, like a car sputtering when running out of gas. My ability to take a breath was the same. The nurses put tubes down my nose to help suck out the yucky mucus blocking my breathing, but it made me have massive nose bleed, but I still couldn't take a breath effectively. I told the nurse I needed help, she got the rapid response team to come and prepare to put me on a ventilator.

My worst fear was that I couldn't move and being put on a ventilator and not being able to do anything. The lead doctor came in and I still didn't want the ventilator, he told me to get it done, or pneumonia was going to settle in and I could die. So, I told them to go ahead and do it. I prayed before I was put under, "Dear Jesus, please take care of my wife and family, I can't do anything, but you have everything under control. Jesus help me to give up and let you take the wheel in my life. I could hear the small voice of God say, "I created you in your mother's womb, and I know all the hairs on your head, I have everything under control."

Matthew 11:28-30 New International Version (NIV)

[28] "Come to me, all you who are weary and burdened, and I will give you rest. [29] Take my yoke upon you and learn from me, for I am gentle and humble in heart, and you will find rest for your souls. [30] For my yoke is easy and my burden is light."

The nurse told me to count to back from 10 to 0, I remember 10,9,8...and out I went, then I felt a peace that passes all understanding, I was under a huge eagle's wings and felt safe, no worries and no anxiety, as I was soaring under the eagle's wings, I saw all different races of people farming and throwing out seeds, all different nationalities. I saw seeds thrown onto different rich soils. God was speaking to my heart," scatter the seeds, keep scattering the seeds, I will provide, keep scattering the seeds to everyone. Then I opened my eyes and I saw my dad and brother, they were there by my bed. I had such a peace that everything was in God's Hands and everything was going to be okay. I couldn't talk and I couldn't move my hands or legs, and my face was sagging.

This Guillain-Barre Syndrome, works from your toes to your head or head to your toes and back again. Meaning, the body thinks its fighting something and doesn't have anything to fight, so it attacks the peripheral nervous system, the myelinated sheaths on your nerve endings and destroys them, so you can't walk, breath, move or do any voluntary movements (gross or detailed fine movements). I physically died, I couldn't do anything, but think, see, and hear.

Praise Jesus, I remember praying to God, to give me the focus and discipline to pray without ceasing and asked God to give me the desire to pray for every medical staff or person that came into my room. I asked God to show me how and when to pray. God is so good. I was in and out all the time, meaning, being asleep and awake, and blurry, but every time I woke up, people were praying over me, around my bed and laying hands on me. God answered prayers through everyone praying for me. Every day, God brought me and my family many visitors and prayer warriors. If I tried to name everyone, I would leave someone out. Thank you to all, for your prayers and encouragement, from me and the Ward Family.

I am a driven and have to have a list to conquer daily. I love to control and organize things. I couldn't do that, I was at "o" Zero-DEAD PHYSICALLY!!!!

Matthew 26:39 New International Version (NIV)

³⁹ Going a little farther, he fell with his face to the ground and prayed, "My Father, if it is possible, may this cup be taken from me. **Yet not as I will, but as you will.**"

SIX
RISE UP

Ephesians 5:14 New International Version (NIV)

¹⁴ This is why it is said:

"Wake up, sleeper,

rise from the dead,

and Christ will shine on you."

From the first night, being on the ventilator, my daughter Kristi would come in at night and stay and read scripture to me for hours and pray and sing to me and hold me. I tear up typing this, God used her, wife (Jan), Lauren, dad, brother, church family, and many others to help me rise up and press on. Kristi would share what God was doing, she told me," God is not only transforming you, but God is transforming the church, community, friends, and many others. The ministerial alliance formed a community prayer evening at our church, and this was when I was on the ventilator. Brother Paul Right organized the prayer meeting, the community cried out for a miracle to happen, healing, and for my family-so powerful. I think about Danny Bolin and David Fernandez, visited me and my family almost every day. The community established a bank account for everyone to donate money to help with gas and meals for my family, and David Fernandez organized it. I thank everyone for their donations, prayers, encouragement, and helping me with (Jan) and family. God has provided for all the needs of family, church, school, and community.

God showed me that He can do anything and nothing is impossible!!

The doctors and neurologists came and checked on me, ran tests, took blood, -and poked and prodded. After being on the ventilator for 3 days, the doctor told them to pull out the ventilator. Here is the moment, the nurse said on the count of three, we are pulling out the ventilator, don't swallow and wait until we suction the yucky stuff before you try to take a breath. One, two, and three, they pulled it out and Praise Jesus, I started breathing on my own. The nurse said this is amazing and a miracle, because most patients that have this syndrome as bad I was, they are on the ventilator for 2 to 6 months.

God is so Good. I was enjoying breathing and being able to speak to my family that I love them and thank everyone. Later that morning, the speech therapist came by to test my swallowing, I haven't eaten for many days. She started with ice chips, I ate and swallowed and then pudding. Wow, it was the greatest pudding I got to eat and Praise Jesus, I ate three to four puddings. It was so awesome, and now they could gradually put me on food. The next 48 hours was so tough, I could not sleep and the withdraws from the propanol, they put you on when on the ventilator. It was tough, I had a hard time breathing for the first 24 hours and man, it was tough dealing with bed sours, and getting comfortable. I know I called on the nurses a million times, they were so awesome. Twenty-four hours after the ventilator, the physical therapists came by and sat me on the edge of the bed, I sat up for eighteen seconds, I couldn't raise my head and move anything. But I could feel more in my toes and hands and wiggle them.

After 11 days in the ICU, they moved me to a private room. The eating got back to normal food, I was gaining a little more strength. The therapists came by and told me that I was going to stand and walk today. I just prayed for God's great strength and courage to walk. They sat me up and I felt like I ran a marathon, then they put the walker in front of me and I grabbed it and all therapists and medical staff helped me up, I could feel they had to lift all of me up. I looked like I was break dancing, legs and arms where wiggling and shaking. I took 10 steps and had to sit down and get back to bed. It was ugly steps, but we did it. I just prayed God would keep getting me stronger. I also prayed about August 2, 2018, it was the date of the FCA Rally, at Albany, TX football field. Mr. Johnson, Coach, FCA director asked me to speak. I remember asking God if I needed to cancel it, felt God tugging me NO, God spoke to my heart that I was going to walk into the Albany Lion Stadium and speak. I laughed out loud and thought how can this happen, but God can do anything.

The next day, Mr. Johnson came by and asked me about it, I told him I will be there to speak and will walk into the stadium. Mr. Johnson said, "Praise Jesus", let's do it. At this time, Coach Casey (Athletic Director and Head Football Coach), my boss, was having hernia surgery and was in a room the floor above me. The therapists came in, I asked them, that I wanted to walk to the elevators and go see and pray with Coach Casey. Coach Casey and his wife (Sabrina) where every day visiting us and helping us. At the time the therapists came in, Brother Paul Wright and his wife came to visit me, and they got me up and I didn't wiggle as much, but took one tough step after the next and got to the elevator and sat in the wheel chair, felt like I played a whole football game. We all went up to see Coach Casey and his wife, and Brother Wright prayed over all of us, it was an awesome tearful time.

We got back to the room and the therapist where impressed and said I was ready for Hendrick Rehab Center, rigorous work. Praise Jesus, the day before, they said I wasn't ready and thought I would stay inpatient rehab in hospital for 4-5 days, but that evening they transported me to the Hendrick Rehab for 2 weeks or more. When I got to the Rehab Center, I could move my arms up to my belly button, no further, I had little grip and always needed help get into bed and to get up out of bed. All the medical staff warned me to be ready to work. I prayed God would give me the strength to do my absolute best and be patient and listen to everyone.

First day, had a rough night of sleep, the occupational therapist came in at 8:00 a.m. with breakfast and put it in front of me and said, "Eat". I told her, I needed help and my wife always fed me. She said, "not anymore, you have to learn", they told me that I will have to learn to walk, dress, eat, and do daily things like a child. Breakfast was an experience, I grabbed the apple juice and couldn't open it, I got frustrated and ripped the juice open and it went all over the place and I pushed it on the floor. The occupational therapist was so patient and awesome. Every day she had a goal for me and was not easy on me. Then the work began, I would work hours with physical therapist and take a break and then occupational therapist, then ate lunch and had hours of therapy after lunch. Man, I was wearing out, but awesome results. I learned to walk with the walker and coordinated movements. I remember laying down, bench pressing a PVC pipe and it felt like 400lbs.

After the first week, I was able to eat breakfast on my own nearly, I could brush my teeth and began taking steps walking down the hall and back with the walker. Every day I was in ICU, hospital, and Hendrick Rehab, I had visitors to encourage and pray for me and the family. Many times, I wanted to feel sorry for myself, but the power of prayer, led me to keep TBN Christian network on tv. I left it on all night and as much as possible, I wanted nothing but Jesus and positive in my eyes and ears. God put it on my heart to be a servant in the situation I was in, God opened up many doors to encourage people rehabbing from stroke, brain surgery, and broken hips, heart surgery, and other challenging illnesses, I was able to pray, love, and encourage everyone and the people that took care of me and the other patients at the rehab. God anointed that time, it gave me great strength and healing.

Second Week, I learned how to take a shower and dress by myself. I started to walk without a walker. I put the walker away to the side. I was able to eat without any assistance. It was awesome to eat a Whataburger, thanks to Jeff Rhoads, who brought me two of them. I remember working in the physical therapy room, trying to lift legs over little hurdles, I got to the last one and collapsed. God showed me what my limit was and respect it and to rest when I was tired. On that Sunday, we had our church," Be Real Prayer Time", in my room, at the Henrick Rehab. It was so Awesome and a God moved in a mighty way. July 17, 2020, Tuesday, they release me to go home. God is so powerful, Jan loaded me into the car and we went back to Stamford, to our house. Home sweet home, it was so peaceful to be home, that evening, Jan set up a surprise homecoming at our church fellowship hall. It was so great, our church family, other church family's, coaches, players, and community, came and celebrated God getting me home. When I got home, Danny Bolin and other deacons made our house handicapped modified, meaning bars in the bathroom shower and house steps, so I could use them to brace and help pull me up and be safe and stable. After the first week at home, I got to put the walker away in storage and get rid of the shower chair. Praise Jesus, I still felt weak and had a long way to go, but God was getting me better. The next couple of weeks, I would use little candles and do my therapy lifting and exercises and I would go to the gym and get on treadmill and walk at the speed of 1.3 to start then 2.0. I would walk 10 min and then sit down and then walk again. Praise Jesus, I got better and better at it.

August 2, 2020-FCA Rally at Albany, Texas, football stadium. I was able to walk onto the field and share the testimony God gave me throughs this 100-0 experience. It was hot but, I praise God for doing the impossible. The next Monday, I started two-a-day workouts, I would coach the defense with a golf cart behind me and then go in and rest in the coach's office and prepare for the next day workouts. I want to say thank you to Coach Casey and all coaches, for taking on extra responsibilities, so I could heal and get better. Dr. Barnett (Supt) and Mr. London (Principal) helped me in the classroom, if I needed to rest or go take a nap or take a day off, they let me do that. Day by day, I got a little stronger. Stamford First Baptist was always there for me and in September voted for me to be the bi-vocational pastor. I am so honored to be able to serve such an awesome church family. God can do anything, I will never see life the same, God transformed me, family, friends, church family, and many others. We will never look at life the same. My wife, Jan, has been my backbone and always by my side with unconditional love. Also, my daughters Kristi, Lauren, and Collins, brother (Don), and dad, always by my side praying and helping. I want to thank all doctors, nurses, medical staff, and therapists for being there for me and always encouraging me to press forward. Thank All of You for Your Love and putting this scripture into action.

John 13:34-35 New International Version (NIV)

[34] "A new command I give you: Love one another. As I have loved you, so you must love one another. [35] By this everyone will know that you are my disciples, if you love one another."

SEVEN
GOD IS IN CONTROL

God has shown me through this journey, that He is in total control. I may think I know what's going on, but in reality, I know nothing.

Isaiah 55:8-9 New International Version (NIV)
⁸ "For my thoughts are not your thoughts,
   neither are your ways my ways,"
declares the Lord.
⁹ "As the heavens are higher than the earth,
   so are my ways higher than your ways
   and my thoughts than your thoughts.

For so many years, I tried to control and work things out myself and include God in the process. God showed my that He has everything worked out and let Jesus drive my life, in all aspects, and get out of the way. God will work everything out for His Glory.

Romans 8:28 New International Version (NIV)

[28] And we know that in all things God works for the good of those who love him, who[a] have been called according to his purpose.

Going through being dead physically and not being able to move my body, forced me to understand about that God has everything worked out. We just need to stay in tune with God and be obedient. God works out the unseen(eternal), He is always working on other people's hearts and working on situations and circumstance that we don't see or understand.

Galatians 2:20 New International Version (NIV)

[20] I have been crucified with Christ and I no longer live, but Christ lives in me. The life I now live in the body, I live by faith in the Son of God, who loved me and gave himself for me.

God knew that I was going to go through this tough test, and God put me in the right hospital, with the proper and greatest medical care. The odds of me getting this syndrome was 1 our of a 100, 000 in the United States. Hendrick Hospital seen a lot of cases of it, I didn't know that, but God did. That is why Wichita Falls Hospital didn't work out, and also Abilene is 40 miles from Stamford and not two hours from Stamford. God knew the outpouring of prayer and support that was needed. God put many people in my life to be encouraged but also for me to encourage and testify about Jesus. I always preached and talked about dying to yourself and be totally surrendered to Jesus. I am so thankful to be able to walk the journey of dying physically and witness a miracle in my life. To be able to witness the powerful God we serve in action. To be able to see a nothing situation, become an only God could do it situation.

NOTHING **IN OUR LIFE HAPPENS BY ACCIDENT OR WITHOUT PURPOSE:**

God knows everything about each of us and knows what hurts us and prospers us. Jeremiah 18 states that God is the potter and we are the clay. The potter designs master pieces and is skilled in every that happens to the clay on the potter's wheel. God will break, mold, and prune every area of our life, to ensure to prepare us for eternal life in heaven with Him. The clay has to have at times a firm steady hand by the potter, pushed and broken by the potter, or transformed by the potters hand.

Psalm 139:13-16 New International Version (NIV)

[13] For you created my inmost being; you knit me together in my mother's womb.

[14] I praise you because I am fearfully and wonderfully made; your works are wonderful. I know that full well.

[15] My frame was not hidden from you when I was made in the secret place; when I was woven together in the depths of the earth.

> **16** Your eyes saw my unformed body; all the days ordained for me were written in your book before one of them came to be.

God knew that John Ward needed to be transformed, by the journey of going through the process of 100-0, from the Gilliam Barre Syndrome. To be died physically, to have faith in the valley of the Sovereign Magnificent God we serve. God has a plan for each of our life, and that plan is under construction till we take our last breath and our heart beats for the last time, and we go with Jesus for eternity.

> **Philippians 1:6** New International Version (NIV)
>
> **6** being confident of this, that he who began a good work in you will carry it on to completion until the day of Christ Jesus.

After getting out of the hospital, starting work, and adapting to normal life. It was so hard mentally. I couldn't go 100 mph like I used to and had to be patient. Nobody could understand the way my body was hurting or the strain it was mentally and physically. It was a battle daily to push it but listen to my body and don't over do it. I would get so tired and battled with any pain and think am I relapsing and going back to the hospital. It has taken over a year to get back to almost normal, I still get fatigued at times quickly and I feel nerve pain and spasms. But God is so faithful, He gives me great strength and desire to press forward. I have such a great amount of gratitude and understand every breath we take is a gift from God.

James 1:2-4 New International Version (NIV)
Trials and Temptations

[a] ² Consider it pure joy, my brothers and sisters, whenever you face trials of many kinds, ³ because you know that the testing of your faith produces perseverance.⁴ Let perseverance finish its work so that you may be mature and complete, not lacking anything.

With this Covid-19 going on, tough time, but God is in control. When we are tested spiritually, mentally, or physically, know God is in control and works everything out for the good. God is always molding us to be stronger in our faith and provides more than we ever need daily. Stay focused on Jesus!!! Keep praying and meditating on God Word and strive to be obedient to God's Word Daily. God will get us through the storms of life, deep valleys, and suffering in our life. God will never leave us or forsake us.

THE CLOSER WE GET TO GOD, THE MORE WE UNDERSTAND GOD'S LOVE AND HOW MUCH GOD IS IN CONTROL, AND THAT WE ARE IN NO CONTROL!!!!

John 3:30 New International Version (NIV)" He must become greater; I must become less."

EIGHT
OVERFLOW

Romans 15:13 New International Version (NIV)

¹³ May the God of hope fill you with all joy and peace as you trust in him, so that you may overflow with hope by the power of the Holy Spirit.

After I got home from the Hendrick Rehab Center, I was filled with an overflow of gratitude and awe of God's power, looking how far God brought me. It was so awesome to feel such an overflow of love and thankfulness. Church family, community, family, and friends overflowed with being servants, we didn't have to cook an evening meal for one or two months. My neighbors mowed our lawn and edged it, I didn't have to mow the lawn for a year. Daily, I felt the overflow of God's strength and healing, every day I felt a little stronger. I look back at the from 100-0, I see God's loving hand and how great of a God we serve. In the rehab, God gave me 12 sermons on the overflow: love, grace, mercy, forgiveness, power, knowledge, courage, strength, wisdom, and many more. I want to share what God taught me through this test and opened my heart about live itself.

First, we are all going to have an overflow of suffering in our life. Life is no rose garden, no matter if we are Christians or not Christians.

Matthew 5:45 New International Version (NIV)

⁴⁵ that you may be children of your Father in heaven. He causes his sun to rise on the evil and the good, and sends rain on the righteous and the unrighteous.

Storms, tribulations, suffering, and deep valleys are going to happen in our life. We need to keep Jesus #1 Priority in our life no matter what we are going through. God gives us strength and joy, to get through those tough times. The key is to keep pressing forward and never look back. Keep striving to become more Christlike.

Philippians 3:12-14 New International Version (NIV)

¹² Not that I have already obtained all this, or have already arrived at my goal, but I press on to take hold of that for which Christ Jesus took hold of me. ¹³ Brothers and sisters, I do not consider myself yet to have taken hold of it. But one thing I do: Forgetting what is behind and straining toward

what is ahead, ¹⁴ I press on toward the goal to win the prize for which God has called me heavenward in Christ Jesus.

Suffering, storms, and tribulation is what molds us, builds Godly character, and gives us great perseverance. In the ICU, on the ventilator, God gave me a great peace and strength daily to focus on Him. When the ventilator was taken off, God gave me a desire to speak God's love to everyone possible and testify how awesome God is. I couldn't write or read the bible at first for a while, but the Holy Spirit brought scriptures to my mind and heart, that is where God gave me the Overflow Series of sermons. God spoke to me through pray, Christian TV Station, encouragement of brothers and sisters of Christ, and medical staff. God is so good and provides immeasurably more than we need.

> **James 1:2-4** New International Version (NIV)
> **Trials and Temptations**
> ² Consider it pure joy, my brothers and sisters, [a] whenever you face trials of many kinds, ³ because you know that the testing of your faith produces perseverance.⁴ Let perseverance finish its work so that you may be mature and complete, not lacking anything.

Second, overflow of God's Grace, is the reason that we can press forward in life and the reason why we can always have hope daily. No matter what we go against or go through in life, God's grace is sufficient.

---

2 Corinthians 12:7-9 New International Version (NIV)

⁷ or because of these surpassingly great revelations. Therefore, in order to keep me from becoming conceited, I was given a thorn in my flesh, a messenger of Satan, to torment me. ⁸ Three times I pleaded with the Lord to take it away from me. ⁹ But he said to me, "My grace is sufficient for you, for my power is made perfect in weakness." Therefore, I will boast all the more gladly about my weaknesses, so that Christ's power may rest on me.

Paul cried out to God three times to take the thorn out of his flesh. God said," My Grace is Sufficient", meaning all we need is grace and we will make it. We don't have to fix it, or find a different plan. God's grace enables us to confess our sin when we fall short, and we receive forgiveness and can press on forward to the goal, which is Jesus. Through this Covid-19, it's the same, its tough and not comfortable and a lot of uncharted waters ahead of us, but God's grace is sufficient. Thus, God takes our weaknesses, tribulation, storms, temptation, and mess ups and makes us stronger if we let go and let God have everything in our life.

Romans 8:28 New International Version (NIV)

[28] And we know that in all things God works for the good of those who love him, who[a] have been called according to his purpose.

Because of Gods amazing grace and mercy, the good, bad, and ugly of our life work together to glorify God, if we keep loving God (prayer and meditate on God's word) and glorify God in all we do. Our God can do anything and takes care of His children.

Finally, overflow of God's strength, everyday God gave me a strength that was beyond my abilities. The strength daily gave me focus, courage, and great endurance. I remember learning to walk again, eat, take a shower, shave, or get dressed. It was so frustrating and physically draining. After I would do anything, I felt like I ran a marathon, or I could sleep sitting up or standing up. Reminded me of an Eagle, strong and huge bird, but very graceful bird. The eagle thrives on soaring in the storms of life. An eagle will use its powerful wings to fly higher than the storm clouds and then soar and soar. That is what God wants us to do, when storms hit in life, don't dwell in self-pity or look to the world to fix the storm. Look to Jesus, and He will give us great strength to focus on Jesus and He will help us soar through the storms of life.

Isaiah 40:28-31 New International Version (NIV)

[28] Do you not know?
Have you not heard?
The Lord is the everlasting God,
 the Creator of the ends of the earth.
He will not grow tired or weary,

and his understanding no one can fathom.
²⁹ He gives strength to the weary

and increases the power of the weak.
³⁰ Even youths grow tired and weary,
and young men stumble and fall;
³¹ but those who hope in the Lord
will renew their strength.
They will soar on wings like eagles;
they will run and not grow weary,
they will walk and not be faint.

In closing, I remember when they put the ventilator in, I was flying under the wings of a great eagle (God), I felt so safe and it was so peaceful. The eagle was powerful and graceful. God is that way in our life daily, if we just keep Jesus number one in all areas of our life. Trust that God has everything in our life under control.

Proverbs 3:5-6 New International Version (NIV)
⁵ Trust in the Lord with all your heart
and lean not on your own understanding;
⁶ in all your ways submit to him,
and he will make your paths straight.[a]

I love this set of scripture, easy to say, but hard to do.

Trust means to everyday strive to come closer to God, by loving him with all our heart, mind, soul, and strength. Trust God no matter if our feelings and emotions are telling us not to trust Him. Trust God even if the suffering and tribulation in life is beyond our understanding; it looks unfair and not right and uncertain. Sounds familiar with the Covid-19, uncertain for what is next. We need to submit every area and aspect in life to Jesus.

James 4:7-8 New International Version (NIV)

[7] Submit yourselves, then, to God. Resist the devil, and he will flee from you. [8] Come near to God and he will come near to you. Wash your hands, you sinners, and purify your hearts, you double-minded.

Submit to God, a river overflow of God's love, grace, mercy, forgiveness, strength, and power will flow through you.

NINE
TRANSFORMATION

We can't change unless inwardly we change, then outwardly we will change. Transformation has too happen inwardly before our actions will change!!

Romans 12:1-2 New International Version (NIV)

A Living Sacrifice

12 Therefore, I urge you, brothers and sisters, in view of God's mercy, to offer your bodies as a living sacrifice, holy and pleasing to God—this is your true and proper worship. **²** Do not conform to the pattern of this world, but be transformed by the renewing of your mind. Then you will be able to test and approve what God's will is—his good, pleasing and perfect will.

Transformation is like metamorphosis, total change inwardly and outwardly into another form. For example, a caterpillar to a butterfly or a tadpole to a frog. Jesus is in the transforming business. One example of many that comes to my heart, is from Saul to Paul.

Acts 9:1-19 New International Version (NIV)
Saul's Conversion

9 Meanwhile, Saul was still breathing out murderous threats against the Lord's disciples. He went to the high priest **2** and asked him for letters to the synagogues in Damascus, so that if he found any there who belonged to the Way, whether men or women, he might take them as prisoners to Jerusalem. **3** As he neared Damascus on his journey, suddenly a light from heaven flashed around him. **4** He fell to the ground and heard a voice say to him, "Saul, Saul, why do you persecute me?"

5 "Who are you, Lord?" Saul asked.

"I am Jesus, whom you are persecuting," he replied. **6** "Now get up and go into the city, and you will be told what you must do."

7 The men traveling with Saul stood there speechless; they heard the sound but did not see anyone. **8** Saul got up from the ground, but when he opened his eyes he could see nothing. So, they led him by the hand into Damascus. **9** For three days he was blind, and did not eat or drink anything.

10 In Damascus there was a disciple named

Ananias. The Lord called to him in a vision, "Ananias!"

"Yes, Lord," he answered.

¹¹ The Lord told him, "Go to the house of Judas on Straight Street and ask for a man from Tarsus named Saul, for he is praying. ¹² In a vision he has seen a man named Ananias come and place his hands on him to restore his sight."

¹³ "Lord," Ananias answered, "I have heard many reports about this man and all the harm he has done to your holy people in Jerusalem. ¹⁴ And he has come here with authority from the chief priests to arrest all who call on your name."

¹⁵ But the Lord said to Ananias, "Go! This man is my chosen instrument to proclaim my name to the Gentiles and their kings and to the people of Israel. ¹⁶ I will show him how much he must suffer for my name."

¹⁷ Then Ananias went to the house and entered it. Placing his hands on Saul, he said, "Brother Saul, the Lord—Jesus, who appeared to you on the road as you were coming here—has sent me so that you may see again and be filled with the Holy Spirit." ¹⁸ Immediately, something like scales fell from Saul's eyes, and he could see again. He got up and was baptized, ¹⁹ and after taking some food, he regained his strength.

WHEN WE ACCEPT Jesus as Lord and Savior in our heart, we become a new creation.

> **2 Corinthians 5:17** New International Version (NIV)
>
> [17] Therefore, if anyone is in Christ, the new creation has come:[a] The old has gone, the new is here!

AS A CHRISTIAN, God gives us the opportunity to transform daily, the key is to saturate ourselves in prayer (communication with God) and meditating on God's Word daily. As we become closer in our walk with God, the more Jesus is in our life. More Jesus in then the more Jesus out. The more world and self in, the more world and self out. What are we looking at with our eyes, what are we allowing in our ears, and who are we hanging out with daily?

The journey of 100-0, from the Oil Bowl, to ICU, to ventilator, and to Hendrick Rehab, and to home. Amazing, God transformed me inwardly, and taught me these key points.

First, God desires and wants all of us, not a little, or half, or some. Jesus wants us to surrender everything to Him. If we think we can hide sin from God, or give only what is comfortable, or act out Christianity, you are dead wrong. God will use circumstances and situations to get us to be totally surrendered to God.

> **Galatians 2:20** New International Version (NIV)
>
> [20] I have been crucified with Christ and I no longer live, but Christ lives in me. The life I now

live in the body, I live by faith in the Son of God, who loved me and gave himself for me.

Look at Paul's life, from persecuting Christians, to when the scales fell from his eyes, to when Paul and Silas were flogged and thrown into prison, to Paul's death. Paul was head of the stoning of Steven and killing Christians and hunting them down. What a transformation for Jesus.

Philippians 3:7-9 New International Version (NIV)

[7] But whatever were gains to me I now consider loss for the sake of Christ. [8] What is more, I consider everything a loss because of the surpassing worth of knowing Christ Jesus my Lord, for whose sake I have lost all things. I consider them garbage, that I may gain Christ [9] and be found in him, not having a righteousness of my own that comes from the law, but that which is through faith in[a] Christ —the righteousness that comes from God on the basis of faith.

Paul went from arrogant and all-knowing, to humble, selfless, and totally content with more or less, as long as he had Jesus. Yes-Amen

God showed me, from the 100-0 journey, that I didn't have to control everything and I didn't have to have Plan B for everything. God just wanted all of me, to include Jesus in every area of my life. Give up, and let God be in control.

Second, perspective of live, seeing life on my back and

totally physically dead, then upright racing through life. Everything looks different on your back, can't move your body, can't talk to anyone, and need help to do anything. Very humbling, go from 100-0 in 24 – 48 hours. God showed me how to see through someone paralyzed, stroke, brain surgery, or anything that strikes you physically and stops you in your stride of life. I praise Jesus for allowing me to walk in their shoes for a duration and deal with uncertainty. Sounds familiar, the Covid-19, look how your life has changed in 3 to 4 weeks. We will all be transformed as a world, nation, states, counties, communities, towns, and individually. We will not be the same. God loves us so much that He desires to transform us daily to be more Christlike, and He is faithful to prepare each of us for eternity.

Finally, power, I was shown how powerful God is, nothing is too hard for Jesus!!!

---

2 Timothy 1:7 New International Version (NIV)
⁷ For the Spirit God gave us does not make us timid, but gives us power, love and self-discipline.

The journey from being dead physically to being upright and living life showed me how powerful God is. I learned, Jesus gives us hope every day. We just need to cry out to God, He will answer and meet all our needs. God gave me peace and joy in the midst of suffering and pure chaos. It seemed like every day was slow and challenging. God would answer and show me how great and powerful He is daily, by little victories and then medium victories and huge victories. God was powerful through people, our family, church family, churches, community, and friends.

Prayer was the power of God in action. Things happened daily that only God could do. God sent encouragement and hope daily. When we go from everything to nothing, God is at His greatest. I also think of Job, in the Bible, a God-fearing man that had a great family, popular, and financially prospering. Job within 24 hours lost his family, money, and physical appearance to boils, and much more. Yet Job kept the faith, ever thou everything looked hopeless to him, his wife told him to curse God and die, and his friends all condemned him. But Job was steadfast and kept the faith and God prospered him more than ever later. I bet Job went through transformation, and Job was never the same.

TEN
VICTORY LIVING

1 Corinthians 15:57 New International Version (NIV)

⁵⁷ But thanks be to God! He gives us the victory through our Lord Jesus Christ.

Being real and authentic is what victory living is. To love God with all our heart, mind, soul, and strength and loving people. Every day we have the opportunity to be victorious in every area of our life, despite circumstances and situations.

Every day at the hospital and rehab was uncharted territory, this sounds familiar with this Covid 19. God taught me to take every day as a blessing to be able to Glorify God in everything and be an influence for Jesus. Every day was a day for victory living.

First, our life is not guaranteed, we don't every know when we will take our last breath or our heat beat its last beat. Only God knows the moment that will happen.

James 4:13-17 New International Version (NIV)
Boasting About Tomorrow

[13] Now listen, you who say, "Today or tomorrow we will go to this or that city, spend a year there, carry on business and make money." [14] Why, you do not even know what will happen tomorrow. What is your life? You are a mist that appears for a little while and then vanishes. [15] Instead, you ought to say, "If it is the Lord's will, we will live and do this or that." [16] As it is, you boast in your arrogant schemes. All such boasting is evil. [17] If anyone, then, knows the good they ought to do and doesn't do it, it is sin for them.

Everyday no matter how tough it was or if I was frustrated and upset, God showed me that live is precious and while we are here on earth, we need to thank Jesus for Victory. Meaning, spend time with Jesus daily in prayer and saturate ourselves in Gods Word. Make every second and breath in our life count for Jesus.

Second, be humble and get rid of the pride. Life is not about self, we need to be selfless. Humble is an easy and awesome word to say, but a battle to live out.

Philippians 2:3-4 New International Version (NIV)

[3] Do nothing out of selfish ambition or vain conceit. Rather, in humility value others above

yourselves, [4] not looking to your own interests but each of you to the interests of the others.

God showed me so much about being humble, journey of dying physically, and everyone having to help me just to live, my pride was thrown out the window. I had to be totally selfless to endure and function through ICU, ventilator, and rehab. To be selfless, we must totally trust God to provide from breathing or anything else. God is in Control. We are to do everything to glorify Jesus!!!

Colossians 3:17 New International Version (NIV)

[17] And whatever you do, whether in word or deed, do it all in the name of the Lord Jesus, giving thanks to God the Father through him.

In life, we need to put the pride to the side and let Jesus do whatever needs to be done in our life. The key is to glorify God in all aspects of our life.

Psalm 32:8-11 New International Version (NIV)

[8] I will instruct you and teach you in the way you should go;

> I will counsel you with my loving eye on you.

[9] Do not be like the horse or the mule,
> which have no understanding
but must be controlled by bit and bridle
> or they will not come to you.

> [10] Many are the woes of the wicked,
> but the Lord's unfailing love
> surrounds the one who trusts in him.
> [11] Rejoice in the Lord and be glad, you righteous;
> sing, all you who are upright in heart!

I had to daily put my emotions, feelings, and self-pity in God's Hands, and it's so awesome what God can do, when we let go and let God. Give God everything in our life.

Third, victory living is putting God's Word into action. Putting God's word into action is being obedient in God's word daily. I love the example, Matt. 7:24-27, states when we obey Gods word and live it, we build our house or life on the Rock. A rock foundation is stable and will not change or shift. The foundation of a house is the most important part of the house. If you have cracks develop in your foundation, big problems will sooner or later totally destruct the house. The rock foundation is Jesus in our life. We must have Jesus first in our life or we will be unstable and chaotic and sooner or later, destruction will take place. If we do not put Gods word into action, we built our house or life on sand. Sand is unstable, shifts in every direction. If our foundation in our life sand and unstable. Thus, we will live life on emotions and feeling, like we are on a roller coaster. Going up and down and around and will not grow closer in our walk with God.

In conclusion, victory living is living for Jesus every moment and every breath. Be humble in every way, glorifying Jesus in all areas of life. Put Gods word into action and built your life on the Rock-Jesus, Jesus, and more Jesus.

ELEVEN
THE MIRACLE

Do miracle's still happen? Yes, everyday around us, we just are blind to them. We are so focused on seeing a green smoke or burning bush. The busyness of this world blinds us from seeing the miracles in front of us. I was one of that got to be a miracle. The Gilliam Barre Syndrome was the test that brought a miracle in my life, I had the syndrome to the worst degree, meaning being put on a ventilator. When I was being put on the ventilator, God showed me what a powerful God we serve. I shared earlier, I was under the mighty wings of a giant eagle, showed me what a sovereign God we serve and God has everything handled. When I woke up till my walking out of rehab, I felt and was the product of hundreds of people, from all over praying for me and my family. It was a miracle to get off the ventilator in 3 days, to walk, to use my hands and legs, getting dressed, take a shower, and do daily tasks. The reason we don't have miracles is because of the lack of faith.

Matthew 13:58 New International Version (NIV)

⁵⁸ And he did not do many miracles there because of their lack of faith. Faith is the trust that God is in control of the uncertain, unseen, and unknown things in our life.

Hebrews 11:1 New International Version (NIV)
Faith in Action

11 Now faith is confidence in what we hope for and assurance about what we do not see.

As Christians, it is so easy to tell or just say we have to have faith, but is so hard to put into action. Especially, when life is chaotic, stormy, and lots of tribulation. Through these times is when God does miracles in our life or things that only God can do. I knew that the only way that I could rehab or get better from the Gilliam Barre Syndrome, was by a miracle from God. Thus, not by my strength, but by God's strength and power through me. We must have faith that God allows circumstances and situations or tests to happen in our life, to mold us, break us, and prune us into the masterpiece He calls us to be.

James 1:2-4 New International Version (NIV)
Trials and Temptations

² Consider it pure joy, my brothers and sisters,

[a] whenever you face trials of many kinds, ³ because you know that the testing of your faith produces perseverance. ⁴ Let perseverance finish its work so that you may be mature and complete, not lacking anything.

When I wanted to quit and throw the towel in, God said no, and brought me visitors and people to encourage me to keep pressing on. Through that special time, from collapsing in my living room floor, ICU, and Rehab, God taught me, molded me, and transformed me to become more Christlike. Praise Jesus!!!! We must have faith, and faith comes from our relationship with God. The more we spend time in prayer and meditate on God's Word, and are obedient to God; the more God strengthens our faith by opening our eyes, mind, and hearts to the Lord. Thus, we recognize how God is working in our life.

To have faith, we must trust, meaning tow the line spiritually. Tow the line, we use as a coach all the time. In sports and off-season, we would push our bodies to complete fatigue, we would tell everyone to tow the line. Meaning, everyone stood at attention and gets totally still and what's for key commands, to execute when they are tired. It's about mental discipline, and the desire to listen and trust the coach and each other. We need to tow the line spiritually, by being disciplined, to trust God even when we don't understand, feel comfortable, or what our emotions and feelings say.

Proverbs 3:5-6 New International Version (NIV)

⁵ Trust in the Lord with all your heart
   and lean not on your own understanding;
⁶ in all your ways submit to him,
   and he will make your paths straight.[a]

Same thing spiritually, be disciplined and react to Jesus, no matter the cost or sacrifice. We will mess up and go through sufferings and consequences, but God will help us be strong and react to God. We need to respond to Jesus, not our self.

---

1 Timothy 4:8 New International Version (NIV)
⁸ For physical training is of some value, but godliness has value for all things, holding promise for both the present life and the life to come.

Discipline is learned by the journey we endure from when we accept Jesus as Lord and Savior, in our hearts till we take our last breath, and spend eternity with Jesus in Heaven. God loves us so much that He disciplines us, just as a father disciplines his children.

Hebrews 12:4-12 New International Version (NIV)
God Disciplines His Children
⁴ In your struggle against sin, you have not yet resisted to the point of shedding your blood. ⁵ And

have you completely forgotten this word of encouragement that addresses you as a father addresses his son? It says,

"My son, do not make light of the Lord's discipline,

    and do not lose heart when he rebukes you,

⁶ because the Lord disciplines the one he loves,

    and he chastens everyone he accepts as his son."[a]

⁷ Endure hardship as discipline; God is treating you as his children. For what children are not disciplined by their father? ⁸ If you are not disciplined—and everyone undergoes discipline—then you are not legitimate, not true sons and daughters at all. ⁹ Moreover, we have all had human fathers who disciplined us and we respected them for it. How much more should we submit to the Father of spirits and live! ¹⁰ They disciplined us for a little while as they thought best; but God disciplines us for our good, in order that we may share in his holiness. ¹¹ No discipline seems pleasant at the time, but painful. Later on, however, it produces a harvest of righteousness and peace for those who have been trained by it.

¹² Therefore, strengthen your feeble arms and weak knees.

MIRACLES HAPPEN or we are able to see them, when we become spiritually disciplined in life. Discipline is not fun at times, but the results grow us to become more Christlike.

In conclusion, miracles can be salvation, healing,

protection, spiritual growth, answered prayer, or anything God driven. God showed me that walking, using my arms and legs, or dressing, my family, and life. It's all a miracle and gift from God.

---

2 Corinthians 9:15 New International Version (NIV)

[15] Thanks be to God for his indescribable gift!

TWELVE
PURPOSE+PASSION

Philippians 2:13 New International Version (NIV)

¹³ for it is God who works in you to will and to act in order to fulfill his good purpose.

Every day we have a chance to display great purpose and passion in our life. The question is, "What drives us every day?", or," What gives us passion in our life daily." Jesus desires for us to live life to the fullest and live life abundantly.

John 10:10 New International Version (NIV)

¹⁰ The thief comes only to steal and kill and destroy; I have come that they may have life, and have it to the full.

God's purpose for us is not to live life in self-pity and negative all the time. God wants us to live life with the purpose of glorifying Him in all we do and have great passion in all we do.

Colossians 3:23 New International Version (NIV)

²³ Whatever you do, work at it with all your heart, as working for the Lord, not for human masters

---

There is no way that I could be able to coach and pastor and be a poach. My daughter Kristi, called me a pouch, meaning being a pastor and coach. God gives me the purpose and passion to do both. The great thing is that both are very similar, all jobs are similar, we are called to glorify God in everything we do. No matter is you are a coach, pastor, waiter, dish washer, policeman, or doctor. God's purpose is for you to glorify him in your jobs daily. If that is our purpose daily, God will give us great passion in what we do. I love coaching and teaching, the opportunity daily to influence young men and young women's lives daily. It is challenging and so rewarding. Every day we all have opportunities to show God's love and speak Godly encouragement in what we do. Our purpose, we are to glorify God in our jobs, family, hobbies, and everything we do.

HOW DO WE ACCOMPLISH THAT?

First, we must put on the full armor of God on daily. A football player doesn't run on the field on game day and have no helmet on. A basketball player doesn't run on the court without a basketball. We can't go out in life without the full armor of God or satan will eat our lunch. Satan comes to kill, steal and destroy our life.

---

1 Peter 5:8 New International Version (NIV)

⁸ Be alert and of sober mind. Your enemy the devil prowls around like a roaring lion looking for someone to devour.

Satan prowls around looking for the ones with half or no armor on daily. Satan wants to feed on the weak. We must be strong In the Lord, put the Full Armor of God on daily. We are in a spiritual battle daily 24-7, day in and day out.

Ephesians 6:10-18 New International Version (NIV)

The Armor of God

¹⁰ Finally, be strong in the Lord and in his mighty power. ¹¹ Put on the full armor of God, so that you can take your stand against the devil's schemes. ¹² For our struggle is not against flesh and blood, but against the rulers, against the authorities, against the powers of this dark world and against the spiritual forces of evil in the heavenly realms. ¹³ Therefore put on the full armor of God, so that when the day of evil comes, you may be able to stand your ground, and after you have done everything, to stand. ¹⁴ Stand firm then, with the belt of truth buckled around your waist, with

the breastplate of righteousness in place, ¹⁵ and with your feet fitted with the readiness that comes from the gospel of peace. ¹⁶ In addition to all this, take up the shield of faith, with which you can extinguish all the flaming arrows of the evil one. ¹⁷ Take the helmet of salvation and the sword of the Spirit, which is the word of God.

¹⁸ And pray in the Spirit on all occasions with all kinds of prayers and requests. With this in mind, be alert and always keep on praying for all the Lord's people.

Our enemy daily is satan, not flesh and blood, or people. Its satan and his demons, it's what we don't see.

FULL ARMOR **of God-Strap it ON!!! Stand Firm!!**
Belt of Truth:

The soldier had to have a tool belt to put his different weapons on and keep everything intact on the uniform(armor). It's the most important part of the full armor.

In our life, truth is the most important.

John 14:6 New International Version (NIV)

⁶ Jesus answered, "I am the way and the truth and the life. No one comes to the Father except through me.

Jesus is the truth in all aspects of our life. This

world has a lot of grey areas and tough to know what is true. It is so important to spend daily time in prayer and meditate on God's Word (Truth).

Hebrews 4:12 New International Version (NIV)
¹² For the word of God is alive and active. Sharper than any double-edged sword, it penetrates even to dividing soul and spirit, joints and marrow; it judges the thoughts and attitudes of the heart.

Everything in our life needs to filter through Jesus and allow Jesus to be in all areas of our life.

Breastplate of Righteousness:

The breastplate protects the vital organs of the heart, lungs, and intestines. Everyday God wants us daily to strive to be more Christlike, to become more righteous.

---

1 Peter 1:13-16 New International Version (NIV)
Be Holy
¹³ Therefore, with minds that are alert and fully sober, set your hope on the grace to be brought to you when Jesus Christ is revealed at his coming. ¹⁴ As obedient children, do not conform to the evil desires you had when you lived in ignorance.¹⁵ But just as he who called you is holy, so be

holy in all you do; **¹⁶** for it is written: "Be holy, because I am holy."[a

---

We fall short of the glory of God daily, we are sinners, and we need Jesus to lavish us with His grace and mercy. But God wants us to daily strive to be more righteous and be obedient to Jesus, because we love Jesus so much. Daily when we strive to become more Christlike, we become closer in our walk with God and protect our heart, just like the breastplate does for a soldier.

Feet Fitted with Readiness:

We all understand the importance of good shoes that fit right and not too small or big. For a soldier, most important to have shoes or boots that fit right and are comfortable, but durable.

---

1 Peter 3:15 New International Version (NIV)

¹⁵ But in your hearts revere Christ as Lord. Always be prepared to give an answer to everyone who asks you to give the reason for the hope that you have. But do this with gentleness and respect,

We need to strive daily to put Jesus Lord (#1) in our hearts and always be ready to give an answer for our hope of glory (Jesus).

---

2 Timothy 3:16-17 New International Version (NIV)

¹⁶ All Scripture is God-breathed and is useful

for teaching, rebuking, correcting and training in righteousness, **17** so that the servant of God[a] may be thoroughly equipped for every good work

Saturate our hearts with Gods word daily, and meditate on the word of God. God's word will transform our hearts and lead us in the way of righteousness.

Shield of Faith:

The shield of a soldier, was what protected the soldier in battle, from arrows or any weapons of the enemy. The shield gave extra protection of the whole body of the soldier. Faith is our shield daily from satan's flaming arrows. We have many arrows sent at us from satan. We must have faith that extinguishes the arrows. Faith is the certainty that God is in control, no matter if I can see God at work or not.

Hebrews 11:1 New International Version (NIV)
Faith in Action
11 Now faith is confidence in what we hope for and assurance about what we do not see.

Our faith is reflective, to our relationship with God, meaning, the closer we get to God the greater our faith will be. When we go through tribulation, storms, and hard times, if we stay focused on Jesus. God does things in our life, that only God can do, and our faith grows and grows. For example, I think about Peter, he was a great fisherman, walked by Jesus daily, and betrayed Jesus three times before the rooster crowed. Wow, then Jesus transformed

Peter into the Rock of the Church, one of the greatest evangelists ever.

HELMET OF SALVATION:

The helmet protects the soldier's brain and head, so important. Our salvation protects our mind. Our mind is so powerful, so it's so important to protect it.

---

2 Corinthians 10:3-5 New International Version (NIV)

³ For though we live in the world, we do not wage war as the world does. ⁴ The weapons we fight with are not the weapons of the world. On the contrary, they have divine power to demolish strongholds. ⁵ We demolish arguments and every pretension that sets itself up against the knowledge of God, and we take captive every thought to make it obedient to Christ.

Our salvation needs to engraved in our hearts and minds. When satan is tempting us in many ways, we must know that we are God's child and that satan can't touch us and using our salvation as a weapon. Its huge, I have felt nothing but condemnation and everyone after me and worldly thoughts swarming my head. I go back to February 14, 1990, in Mims auditorium, at Howard Payne University, when I accepted Jesus as Lord and Savior, in my heart. I became a child of God, a new creation in Christ, all the old was wiped away and became a new creation.

> **Romans 8:1** New International Version (NIV)
> **Life Through the Spirit**
> **8** Therefore, there is now no condemnation for those who are in Christ Jesus,

In temptation, speak the moment of salvation in your life and claims Victory in Jesus over the temptation. In the name of Jesus, there is no condemnation, only grace and mercy.

SWORD of the Spirit (God's Word):

God's word is powerful and is our sword in spiritual battle daily. A soldier knows his sword and the strengths and weaknesses of the sword, because the soldier trains daily with the sword to be able to be great and affective in battle.

> **Psalm 119:97-105** New International Version (NIV)
> מ *Mem*
> ⁹⁷ Oh, how I love your law!
>   I meditate on it all day long.
> ⁹⁸ Your commands are always with me
>   and make me wiser than my enemies.
> ⁹⁹ I have more insight than all my teachers,
>   for I meditate on your statutes.
> ¹⁰⁰ I have more understanding than the elders,
>   for I obey your precepts.

¹⁰¹ I have kept my feet from every evil path
   so that I might obey your word.
¹⁰² I have not departed from your laws,
   for you yourself have taught me.
¹⁰³ How sweet are your words to my taste,
   sweeter than honey to my mouth!
¹⁰⁴ I gain understanding from your precepts;
   therefore I hate every wrong path.
ב *Nun*
¹⁰⁵ Your word is a lamp for my feet,
   a light on my path.

GOD'S WORD is so important in our life, we need to meditate on God's word day and night, and apply it in all areas of our life. I love Beth Moore's book, "Praying God's Word", it is so powerful, we must know God's work, just like a soldier needs to know his sword. Ask the Holy Spirit to engrain God's word on your heart and show you how to apply it in your life. Most important, put God's word into action, be obedient and honor God.

Joshua 1:8-9 New International Version (NIV)

⁸ Keep this Book of the Law always on your lips; meditate on it day and night, so that you may be careful to do everything written in it. Then you will be prosperous and successful. ⁹ Have I not commanded you? Be strong and courageous. Do not be afraid; do not be discouraged, for

the Lord your God will be with you wherever you go."

If we are in God's word daily and meditating on it. We will grow closer to God and more Jesus will flow out of us. The key is to put God's word into action, like a soldier uses his sword in battle.

Psalm 1
¹ Blessed is the one
>   who does not walk in step with the wicked
> or stand in the way that sinners take
>   or sit in the company of mockers,
>
> ² but whose delight is in the law of the Lord,
>   and who meditates on his law day and night.
>
> ³ That person is like a tree planted by streams of water,
>   which yields its fruit in season
> and whose leaf does not wither—
>   whatever they do prospers.
>
> ⁴ Not so the wicked!
>   They are like chaff
>   that the wind blows away.
>
> ⁵ Therefore the wicked will not stand in the judgment,
>   nor sinners in the assembly of the righteous.
>
> ⁶ For the Lord watches over the way of the righteous,
>   but the way of the wicked leads to destruction.

Prayer in All Occasions

Last but most important, we need to be prayer warriors. We need to pray without ceasing, through the rough, tough, and great times. Prayer is just talking to God, we need to always no matter what keep talking to God. The more we talk to God, the more we become closer to God and love Him.

Philippians 4:4-7 New International Version (NIV)

Final Exhortations

[4] Rejoice in the Lord always. I will say it again: Rejoice! [5] Let your gentleness be evident to all. The Lord is near. [6] Do not be anxious about anything, but in every situation, by prayer and petition, with thanksgiving, present your requests to God. [7] And the peace of God, which transcends all understanding, will guard your hearts and your minds in Christ Jesus.

God gives us all we need to stand up in Victory for Jesus. The worst thing we can do is do nothing. Meaning, just float along in life and just let things go and just coast spiritually in life. We are either living or dying in spiritually in life. A plant needs water and soil(food) to survive. We must have the Word of God and Prayer daily in our life to survive. Stand up for Jesus with the Full Armor of God on Daily and Fight the Fight.

> **1 Corinthians 15:57-58** New International Version (NIV)
>
> ⁵⁷ But thanks be to God! He gives us the victory through our Lord Jesus Christ.
>
> ⁵⁸ Therefore, my dear brothers and sisters, stand firm. Let nothing move you. Always give yourselves fully to the work of the Lord, because you know that your labor in the Lord is not in vain.

In our times with Covid-19, loss in the family, health problems, marriage problems, and just living life. We need to put the full armor on daily and let Jesus drive every aspect of our life.

THIRTEEN
GOD IS SO GOOD-ALL THE TIME HE IS GOOD

Romans 8:28 New International Version (NIV)

28 And we know that in all things God works for the good of those who love him, who[a] have been called according to his purpose.

What God has Done in My Life:
• February 14, 1990-God chose me to be in His kingdom, I accepted Jesus into my heart, as Lord and Savior of my life. I became a child of God and new creation in Christ. Started the greatest adventurous journey with Jesus.

• December 12, 1992-Married the woman God brought me to spend my life with. After 27 years of marriage, she is my backbone and number one fan in my life. We thank God for the many valleys, mountain tops, and tough times in our marriage. God molded us stronger and stronger.

• My mom, dad, memaw, and brother know Jesus as Lord and Savior. God showed me his forgiving power with my stepmother Unok, she had a tough time taking on two rowdy high energy teenagers as my brother and I. We all didn't start out on the right foot and a lot of negativity and resentment was stored up in our hearts. After I became a Christian, God convicted me about forgiving and getting things right with my step mother.

One summer, I went to visit my dad and went to the house and knocked and Unok answered the door, I prayed God would give me courage, strength, and the words to say. Our eyes met, I started to shed tears and asked her for forgiveness for the bad things I done and bad thoughts I had toward her. She started crying and asked for forgiveness and who it felt like a 1,000lb weight was taken off my chest. Our relationship from that point on was awesome. She got real sick with her lungs and was on oxygen all the time and died not long after that time. But, I went to visit them, when my grandfather past away and she was so excited to tell me, she accepted Jesus as Lord and Savior. Praise Jesus, I will see Unok again. God grew us all closer to Him. God done things that only God could do, I witnessed transformation.

- January 22, 1996-My oldest daughter, Lauren Jane Ward was born in Sulphur Springs, Tx, it was a complete miracle. Seeing the fingers and toes and the magnificent creation of God.

- January 12, 1998-My youngest daughter, Kristi Elizabeth Ward, was born in Brownwood, Tx. Wow, God is so Good. Again, God's miraculous Creation.

- Praise Jesus for the 25 plus years of coaching/teaching and being involved with FCA. God has blessed my whole family and brought so many kids and people that we were able to plant seeds in lives. We have been able to be in a lot of different places for great reasons and purpose.

- Praise Jesus for the 18 plus years of bi-vocational ministry. It's been such a blessing to be able to serve in school systems, church families and communities. We have been so Blessed to serve in many places.

• March 3, 2014-My granddaughter, Collins Faith Ward, was born at Sweetwater, Tx. I got to be the first person to hold her and have been by her side ever since. She is a miracle and God put her in our life for more reasons I could every write down.

• April 4, 2014-My dad married JoAnne (Memaw), I had the blessing of doing the ceremony. Memaw is a God sent to my dad and all our family.

• June 17, 2018-I was blessed with the Guillain Barre Syndrome, one of the toughest and roughest time in my life. God was stronger and blessed me with a miracle. Praise Jesus, for my wife (Jan), Daughters (Kristi, Lauren, Collins), First Baptist Church Family, Ministerial Alliance, Churches, Stamford Community, and friends, coaches, and brothers and sisters in Christ from all over the state and parts all over the United States. Thank You Jesus for all doctors, nurses, therapists, and medical staff at Hendrick Hospital (ICU, etc) and also Hendrick Rehab.

• July 27, 2019-Kristi E. Ward got married to Andrew Norwood. God blessed us with a Christian Son-in-Law. Thank you, Jesus, for allowing me to be a part of an awesome wedding and seeing Kristi so happy.

• November 15, 2019- my grandson was born, Easton James Norwood, was born in Hendrick Hospital, in Abilene Tx. Gods awesome creation, and such a blessing seeing Kristi and Andrew being great parents. It's a joy to observe great Christian parents.

• Thank you, Jesus, for everything, every breath, and every test in all my life to this point. I know many more tests and suffering will happen in my life before I take my last breath and go spend eternity with Jesus. I praise Jesus for the times that were so tough that I didn't want to go another step or minute or take another breath, but God is faithful and bigger and got us through it, and become my Christlike through it all.

• Thank Jesus for all the mentors, friends, coaches, kids, churches, FCA, and many others that were part of times in my life. God knew the timing and the needs that need to be met in my life and my families life.

• Thank you to my wife's parents: Bryan Boyd(BB) and Janie Boyd and family for always being there for me and my family. They have always been faithful in prayer and support. Janie and BB were there by my side in the hospital, taking care of kids , whatever it took, and mighty prayer warriors. Thank you to Chris, Dana, Bryce, Brady, and Brock for prayers and support.

ABOUT THE AUTHOR

My name is John Anthony Ward; God has blessed me to be a teacher and coach at Dublin ISD. For twenty-eight years, I have been a teacher and coach. For most of those years, God has used me as a bi-vocational pastor. My youngest daughter calls me Poach, meaning coach and pastor. God has given me and my family strength and the passion to do both. I want to thank coach Jimmy Keeling and Dr. Don Newberry for helping me to put this book together and giving great encouragement to write this book. The Ward family's prayer is that God will plant great seeds of encouragement for every one that reads this book. I thank God for all the people God has put in my life and my families life that have helped us to this day: family, church families, friends, and many more.

DON'T TAKE FOR GRANTED ANY TIME WITH FAMILY, FRIENDS, AND LOVED ONES!!!!

James 4:13-17

New International Version

Boasting About Tomorrow

¹³ Now listen, you who say, "Today or tomorrow we will go to this or that city, spend a year there, carry on business and make money." ¹⁴ Why, you do not even know what will happen tomorrow. What is your life? You are a mist that appears for a little while and then vanishes. ¹⁵ Instead, you ought to say, "If it is the Lord's will, we will live and do this or that." ¹⁶ As it is, you boast in your arrogant schemes. All such boasting is evil. ¹⁷ If anyone, then, knows the good they ought to do and doesn't do it, it is sin for them.

May God Bless Everyone,

John Anthony Ward

Made in United States
Orlando, FL
09 September 2022

22189184R10057